The real thing?

The real thing?

A book to help you examine yourself

An abridged version, written for today's readers, of the classic
Distinguishing Traits of Christian Character by Gardiner Spring, 1829; a
revision of the book *What's real?* published by Grace Publications, 1978.
Translations have been published in Tamil and Spanish.

Grace Publications

© Grace Publications Trust
139 Grosvenor Avenue
London N5 2NH
England

Joint Managing Editors
   J. P. Arthur, M.A.
   H. J. Appleby

ISBN 0 946462 30 5

Distributed by
EVANGELICAL PRESS
12 Wooler Street
Darlington
Co. Durham DL1 1RQ
England

Cover design and art work: L. L. Evans

Contents

Quotations from the Bible are taken from The Revised Authorized Version, published by Samuel Bagster and Sons Ltd, 1982.

Part One

Counterfeit Christianity!

Know-alls

Sometimes you meet people who seem to know everything. They are always putting everyone else right. They have all the answers (or think they have) and you know nothing (or so they say). With them around, you just cannot win. But even if they are right, and really do know right from wrong, this does not prove that they themselves are doing what is right. Merely knowing facts about Christianity does not make you into a Christian. You may know that something is true and still hate it, or know that something is wrong and still do it; but Christ's people not only know the truth but also love it. The devil himself knows more about God than most people do, but that does not make him a Christian! Knowing is not enough.[a]

The Bible tells us about the kind of people who know all the time that there is a God, and yet refuse to acknowledge him as their God, or to thank him for all that he is and does.[b] Knowledge does not make them into Christians. Of course, knowledge matters: you cannot love a person you do not know; you cannot obey an order you have not heard; you cannot be a Christian without knowing some of the truths of Christianity. You have to know what is right before you can love it.[c] But knowing and loving are two different things. The devil knows God, but he does not love the God he knows: he just goes on doing whatever he wants.[d] It is possible to go to hell with a mind full of facts about heaven. Knowing everything does not prove you have the life of God in you.

a	James 2:19	You believe that there is one God. You do well. Even the demons believe — and tremble!
b	Romans 1:21,22	... because, although they know God, they did not glorify him as God, nor were thankful, but became futile in their thoughts, and their foolish hearts were darkened. Professing to be wise, they became fools ...
c	John 17:3	And this is eternal life, that they may know you, the only true God, and Jesus Christ whom you have sent.
d	1 Corinthians 8:2,3	And if anyone thinks that he knows anything, he knows nothing yet as he ought to know. But if anyone loves God, this one is known by him.

9

Religious people

So who are the real Christians? Perhaps they're the religious people, the sort who have been baptised, confirmed and married in church, and expect to be buried by the church as well. Surely they are Christians, because they have been through all the right ceremonies.[a]

Or are they? Going into a garage and getting oily does not make you into a car, so why should going into church and getting wet make you into a Christian? The Jews we read about in the Bible were very religious people: they went through all the right ceremonies, they went to worship God at the right times and in the proper places, they said their prayers every day, and they gave to charity. But they also nailed Jesus to a cross because they did not want to believe what he told them: which proves that being religious and being one of Christ's people are two different things.[b]

People go to church for all sorts of reasons: out of habit, or because they enjoy the company of the people they meet there, or because they like stained-glass windows and organ music, or because their conscience tells them they ought to, or because they think it is the way to make themselves Christians.

Of course, real Christians go to church as well, not to become Christians, but because they are Christians. They go to keep their souls healthy, for just as strong bodies are built up through good food and drink, exercise and work, so strong souls are built up by the Bible, worship, prayer, praise and Christian fellowship.[c] If we have God's life in us, we will want to go to the place where that life can be built up and kept healthy; but just being there does not prove we have the life. God is not tricked: he does not look to see where we are so much as what kind of people we are.[d]

a	Romans 10:3	For they being ignorant of God's righteousness, and seeking to establish their own righteousness, have not submitted to the righteousness of God.
b	John 16:2,3	They will put you out of the synagogues; yes, the time is coming that whoever kills you will think that he offers God service. And these things they will do to you because they have not known the Father nor me.
c	Psalm 119:103	How sweet are your words to my taste, sweeter than honey to my mouth!
d	1 Samuel 16:7	For the Lord does not see as man sees; for man looks at the outward appearance, but the Lord looks at the heart.

Talkative people

Some people just love talking. It is as if you can just switch them on, and off they go, with a speech on economics, politics, the state of the world, or anything else you care to name, including religion. This is another kind of life that you might mistake for the life God gives: the life of the man who is an expert speaker about religion. But the fact of the matter is that being a good preacher does not prove you are a real Christian.

For example, there is a story in the Bible about a donkey that started to speak, but that did not make it into a man; it remained a donkey![a] The Bible also says a great deal about false prophets, who preach in a way that persuades many men to believe them; but however persuasive they are, they remain false prophets. Fine speaking does not make what you say true. Jesus said that many people who have spent their lives preaching and working in his name will be amazed when he comes back to earth, because he will not recognize them. They never had the life God gives. If you heard them talk you would think they were his people, but they are not.[b]

What this shows is that talking about Christianity does not make people into Christians. Some real Christians are very shy when it comes to talking, but that does not stop them being real. On the other hand, you may pray like a saint, preach like an angel, and still be like a demon inside. Talking is not the same as living, and Christianity is matter a of life, not talk.[c]

a	Numbers 22:28	Then the Lord opened the mouth of the donkey, and she said to Balaam, 'What have I done to you, that you have struck me these three times?'
b	Matthew 7:22,23	Many will say to me in that day, 'Lord, Lord, have we not prophesied in your name, cast out demons in your name, and done many wonders in your name?' And then I will declare to them, 'I never know you; depart from me, you who practise lawlessness!'
c	2 Corinthians 11:3,4	But I fear, lest somehow, as the serpent delivered Eve by his craftiness, so your minds may be corrupted from the simplicity that is in Christ. For if he who comes preaches another Jesus whom we have not preached, or if you receive a different spirit which you have not received, or a different gospel which you have not accepted, you put up with it well.

Feeling sorry

Some people always seem to get things wrong. You can be certain that when they are around, something unexpected will happen. They do not mean to be difficult, and they are always sorry afterwards. It can make them miserable or depressed. They know what it is like to be sorry — for themselves.

The church affects some people like that: it makes them feel sorry for themselves. They hear what the Bible says, and they know that they have not obeyed it. Perhaps they have tried, but they have still got it wrong. They just cannot manage to love God and their neighbour with everything they have, and so they begin to feel sorry for themselves. Perhaps they even admit that they are sinners.

But feeling sorry does not make you into a Christian. Christians do talk about sin and being sorry for it, but they also talk about repenting. Repenting is quite different from feeling sorry for yourself. After all, you can quite easily feel sorry about some sin, and still love it. You can confess some sin, and then go and commit it again. But repenting means stopping doing the thing you are sorry for. Just feeling sorry does not change anything.[a]

---

a   2 Corinthians 7:10   For godly sorrow produces repentance to salvation, not to be regretted; but the sorrow of the world produces death.

12

Being sure!

Some people are convinced they are Christians, and that's that! You just cannot argue with them.

Now it is perfectly true that real Christians are sure they are Christ's people; but there are many people who are sure when they have no right to be, people who think they are so good they must be Christians. After all, they say, they never hurt anyone, they try their best to be good: they must be good enough for God.[a] But it is quite possible to feel sure and be completely wrong. It happens all the time: we all make mistakes. Feeling sure is not the same as being right.[b]

We all have feelings of sorrow, trust, hope, joy, and so on, and at first sight it might appear that the feelings non-Christians have are exactly the same as those Christians have. But if they are not the real thing, you cannot rely on them to last all through your life; and you cannot rely on them to stand you in good stead after death. Being sure for the wrong reasons is completely useless.[c]

According to the Bible, God is not satisfied with anything less than what is perfect, and our lives are not perfect. We may not be as bad as some people we know, but we are a lot worse than God wants us to be, and he is not satisfied with us; and if God is not satisfied with us, we are not Christians.

Christians are people who have had an injection of God's new life. If we show the signs of that new life we can be sure we are Christians: not that we are perfect, but God's new life in us is perfect.[d]

a	Matthew 7:21	Not everyone who says to me, 'Lord, Lord,' shall enter the kingdom of heaven, but he who does the will of my Father in heaven.
b	Job 27:8	For what is the hope of the hypocrite, though he may gain much, if God takes away his life?
c	1 Samuel 15:20,23	And Saul said to Samuel, 'But I have obeyed the voice of the Lord, and gone on the mission on which the Lord sent me .. Then Samuel said, 'Has the Lord as great delight in burnt offerings and sacrifices, as in obeying the voice of the Lord? Behold, to obey is better than sacrifice, and to heed than the fat of rams. For rebellion is as the sin of witchcraft, and stubbornness is as iniquity and idolatry! Because you have rejected the Word of the Lord, he has also rejected you from being king!
d	2 Corinthians 5:17	Therefore, if anyone is in Christ, he is a new creation; old things have passed away; behold, all things have become new.

14

Converts

Some people get very excited about all sorts of things. They are stirred into tremendous activity in support of some worthy cause. They are the visionaries who always seem a bit strange to the rest of us ordinary people. The cause they believe in is more important than anything else, and they can tell you exactly when and where they joined it.

Some Christians are exactly like that. They can tell you exactly when, where and how they became Christians, and they reckon that that proves they really are Christians. But what about those who cannot talk like that? Many Christians cannot tell you when they began to be Christians. You know you are alive, but you do not remember being born; they know they have God's life in them, but they do not know how they got it.[a] Knowing the date an apple tree was planted does not prove it is an apple tree; but the fruit on it does. Knowing the date of some great spiritual experience does not make you a Christian; but having God's life does.[b]

| a | John 3:8 | The wind blows where it wishes, and you hear the sound of it, but cannot tell where it comes from and where it goes. So is everyone who is born of the Spirit. |
| b | Matthew 7:16 | You will know them by their fruits. Do men gather grapes from thorn bushes or figs from thistles? |

Part Two

Look for the signs!

Three types of sign!

Good people, know-alls, religious people, talkative people, people who feel sorry for themselves, people who are sure of themselves, and converts: you might think any or all of these people are Christians; but as we have looked at them, we have found that none of them has the real thing, the life of God in a person that makes them into a Christian. That is why, as we said in the first page, we need to be so careful when we examine ourselves.

You would not set out on a sea voyage if you knew the ship was going to sink; and if you are setting out on the Christian life, or if you think you are already living it, you want to be sure you will stay afloat. You want to know the truth about yourself now, and not when the ship goes down. It would be better to weep over your condition now than to be left to do so in hell, when it is too late. So in the first part of the book, I have attempted to help you to be honest with yourself. There is such a thing as a false hope, when we say, 'I hope everything will be all right', and in fact we do not know. If that is the only hope we have now, we shall have no hope at all when we come to face God.

But there is also such a thing as a true, spiritual hope, which God gives to people, a hope that lives for ever, because God lives for ever.[a] What kind of hope do you have? The Lord Jesus told a story about a man who thought he was secure, but whose hope was totally without foundation.[b] Do not be like him.

Every road has road-signs, and they help you to reach your destination. There are three types of road-sign in England. There are round ones, which are compulsory: they must be obeyed. There are triangular ones, which are advisory: it is safer to take notice of what they say. And there are square ones, which are informative: they give you useful information. In the same way there are three types of sign that show if a person is a real Christian. There are the compulsory signs, which show what our relationship to God is really like: these are loving God, hating sin, and believing Christ. There are the advisory signs, which show the kind of life we have in ourselves: these are humbling ourselves, denying ourselves, and giving ourselves. Then there are the informative signs, which show to people around us that we are Christians: praying, sharing, separating, growing, and obeying. Let us look at each of these in turn ...

a	1 Peter 1:3	Blessed be the God and Father of our Lord Jesus Christ, who ... has begotten us again to a living hope ...
b	Matthew 7:26,27	... a foolish man built his house on the sand: and the rain descended, the floods came, and the winds blew and beat on that house and it fell. And great was the fall.

Loving God (compulsory)

It is normal for children to love their parents. If they do not, something must have gone wrong in their family life. Loving God is a sign that we really are his children, and there is something badly wrong with us if we do not.

Now loving God is not soppy and sentimental. It is tough. It means being convinced he is great. It means being delighted with what he says about himself. It means being keen on what he wants. It means being grateful for all that he has done.

Listen to what one great man of God once said: 'Who is like you, O Lord, among the gods? Who is like you — glorious in holiness, fearful in praises, doing wonders?'[a] In other words, 'God is the greatest!' But you could say that without being pleased about it. That is why we have to say that loving God also includes being delighted that he is great.[b] But again, you could be delighted for the wrong reasons. For example, you could be delighted he is great because you hope to get something out of him. That is why we have to say that loving God also involves being keen on what he wants. But you could be keen on what he wants without also being grateful for it. So we have to say that loving God also includes being grateful for all he does.

Loving God, then, means being convinced and delighted that he is great enough to do whatever he wants, and being so keen on what he wants that you can thank him for everything, even when it is not what you expected or wanted.[c] Most people do not think of him like that. Either they do not know about him, or they do not care about him, or they hate him. Whatever the reason, loving God is the last thing they would think of doing. Anyone who does love God only does so because he has in him a new kind of life, the life God gives.

One of the signs that the life of God has come into a person is the fact that he begins to love God. And that is only what you would expect, because the life God gives must love the God who gave it.[d] For some Christians this means giving up everything rather than giving up God. Some Christians have died for God, in days gone by and in our own day as well.[e] But he does not expect that of most of his people. Very few of them have to die for him. What he does expect is they will all live for him. And living for him means loving him.

Do you love God? Are you convinced that he is the greatest? Are you delighted by that? Are you keen on what he wants? Are you grateful for what he does?[f]

a	Exodus 15:11	Who is like you, O Lord, among the gods? Who is like you, glorious in holiness, fearful in praises, doing wonders?
b	Luke 1:46,47	And Mary said, 'My soul magnifies the Lord and my spirit has rejoiced in God my Saviour'.
c	Ephesians 5:20	Giving thanks always for all things to God the Father in the name of our Lord Jesus Christ.
d	1 John 4:19	We love him because he first loved us.
e	Revelation 12:11	... they did not love their lives to the death.
f	2 Corinthians 5:15	... and he died for all, that those who live should live no longer for themselves, but for him who died for them and rose again.

Hating sin (compulsory)

We have already seen that loving God means being keen on what he wants. One of the things that God is keen on is destroying sin. He hates sin, and expects his people to hate it too.[a] Sin is refusing to obey God's laws. Everybody does it, but that does not alter the fact that God has said that anyone who breaks his law is heading for death; for God is the source of all life, and his laws give life. Break them, and you will be punished with death.[b] Anyone who understands this becomes very sorry, and that is good, as far as it goes. But it does not go far enough. A person must also learn to hate sin itself, and to repent.

Repentance is part of the new life God gives to his people. No human being can repent without God's help: the most anyone can do is to feel sorry they have been found out. But that isn't repentance. Repentance is more than patching up our lives, and hoping everything will be all right.[c] Repentance means hating sin because it is against God, hating ourselves because we are against God, and working hard to stop sinning against God.[d][e]

Remember, repenting means much more than feeling sorry because the results of sin are unpleasant. That is the ordinary human feeling of feeling sorry for ourselves. But when we repent we hate sin because it involves sneering at God's law, ignoring his goodness, and fighting against his work. Repentance means being horrified at the thought of fighting against God.

The result of feeling like that is that you also begin to hate anything that leads you into sin. If you have God's new life in you, you will begin to hate your old life without God, and to be very sorry you ever fought against God. Anyone who has God's pure life in him will begin to feel very dirty and very small.[f]

Listen to what one man said about himself: 'O my God: I am too ashamed and humiliated to lift up my face to you, my God; for our iniquities have risen

22

higher than our heads and our guilt has grown up to the heavens'.[g] Anyone who really feels like that will want to do something to repair all the damage caused by his old life, and will want to struggle as hard as possible to avoid sinning in the same way in the future. If there is no struggle against sin, there is no hatred of sin: we are only sorry about the consequences. Sinners in hell are sorry too, not because they have sinned against God, but because they have found out, too late, that they have sinned against themselves.

Do you hate sin? If so, in what way? Because it hurts you or because it insults God? Do you care when God's law is broken? Do you care when you break it? Have you discovered how rotten your old nature really is? Are you shocked when you realise how many different ways that rottenness shows in your life?[h] Do you build defences against sin when you find a weak place in your life where sin gets in too easily? Have you ever been brokenhearted because you have offended God?[i]

a	Proverbs 8:13	The fear of the Lord is to hate evil; pride and arrogance and the evil way and the perverse mouth I hate.
b	Romans 6:23	For the wages of sin is death, but the gift of God is eternal life in Christ Jesus our Lord.
c	2 Corinthians 7:10	For godly sorrow produces repentance to salvation, not to be regretted; but the sorrow of the world produces death.
d	Psalm 51:4	Against you, you only, have I sinned, and done this evil in your sight.
e	1 Thessalonians 1:9	...how you turned to God from idols to serve the living and true God.
f	Job 42:6	...Therefore I abhor myself, and repent in dust and ashes.
g	Ezra 9:6	O my God: I am too ashamed and humiliated to lift up my face to you, my God; for our iniquities have risen higher than our heads, and our guilt has grown up to the heavens.

| h | Romans 7:18 | For I know that in me (that is, my flesh) nothing good dwells; for to will is present with me, but how to perform what is good I do not find. |
| i | Psalm 51:17 | The sacrifices of God are a broken spirit, a broken and a contrite heart — these, O God, you will not despise. |

Believing Christ (compulsory)

Seeing is more than having eyes: it means using them. Believing is more than knowing: it means using your knowledge, and trusting that it is right. Believing is also more than feeling, because you can feel a thing deeply and still be wrong; feelings are not to be trusted. Believing is trusting what you know without worrying too much what your feelings are.[a]

Believing Christ is relying on him, accepting whatever the Bible says about him, and living on the basis that what he says is true. Believing means learning about him, loving what you learn and in the light of that, living in a way that shows you know there is no one in the world as great as he is.[b] This sort of belief has a special name: 'faith'.

When someone discovers they do not love God as they ought, they feel wretched. They hate the things that stop them loving God, and they admit that God would be quite within his right to punish them with death, in hell. Feeling like this is not natural, but comes from having God's new life in you. And this new life also makes a person able to believe Christ. So people without God's new life cannot believe Christ, and do not want to.

But the person who has the life of God in him finds that after being made to feel wretched there is an invitation, indeed, a command, to come back to God.[c] That person finds that he wants to trust Christ, and rely on him absolutely, and finds he can. For when Christ died on the cross, he took the punishment of the sins of his people, so that they will never have to face that punishment themselves.[d] When a person knows that God will punish sin, he gets afraid; but when he understands that Christ took the punishment instead, he finds that Jesus Christ is wonderful, because he is exactly what he needs.[ef] God's new life in him started by making him feel wretched, but now it pushes him to Christ. He trusts Christ to save from the punishment his sins deserve.[g] He stops being afraid of God. He begins to live his life in a way which shows that he owes his whole escape from punishment to Christ alone. He does not try to gain God's favour by living in a right way, but instead he wants to show how much he appreciates what Christ has done by obtaining God's favour for him.[h]

That is what faith is. That is what Christians mean by believing in Christ, but you cannot do it unless God's Holy Spirit has put new life into you. Faith in Jesus Christ proves that God's life is in you. It's the real thing.[i]

a	Hebrews 11:13	These all died in faith, not having received the promises, but having seen them afar off, they were assured of them, embraced them, and confessed that they were strangers and pilgrims on the earth.
b	John 4:42	Now we believe, not because of what you said, for we have heard for ourselves and know that this is indeed the Christ, the Saviour of the world.
c	Matthew 11:29	Take my yoke upon you and learn from me, for I am gentle and lowly in heart, and you will find rest for your souls.
d	John 3:16	For God so loved the world that he gave his only begotten Son, that whoever believes in him should not perish but have everlasting life.
e	Romans 5:8	But God demonstrates his own love towards us, in that while we were still sinners, Christ died for us.
f	1 John 4:19	We love him because he first loved us.
g	1 John 1:9	If we confess our sins, he is faithful and just to forgive us our sins and to cleanse us from all unrighteousness.
h	Galatians 2:16	... knowing that a man is not justified by the works of the law but by faith in Jesus Christ, even we have believed in Christ Jesus, that we might be justified by faith in Christ and not by the works of the law; for by the works of the law no flesh shall be justified.
i	Galatians 2:20	... it is no longer I who live, but Christ lives in me.

Humbling ourselves (advisory)

So far we have been looking at the compulsory signs, which show what our relationship to God is really like: if they are missing, then you are not one of Christ's people.[a] We come next to the advisory signs, which show the kind of life we have in ourselves. These signs are the proof that we have the compulsory ones.[b] The first advisory sign is humbling ourselves.

Being humble means having the right idea about ourselves. Usually we think we are better than we really are[c], but Christ's people know they did not deserve anything but punishment from God. They know they have to depend entirely on him to give them every bit of goodness they have[d], and so they are willing to let God do whatever he wants with them. It is better to be God's doormat in heaven than a prince in hell.[e]

However, you cannot be humble before God in this way, and be proud as you move among other people. In fact, what you do among your fellow human beings may well give a clue to what you are before God. If you can be humble among other people, whom you can see, then it is possible you may be humble before God, whom you cannot see. Of course, if you are only acting humble with them, then you may be acting before God as well.

If you know anything about real humility, you can be pretty sure that it means God has given you his new life. People are not normally humble like this: they prefer to stand tall and make everyone think they are big.

The Bible says there is more hope for a fool than for a proud man.[f] People have sometimes called Christians 'fools'. Perhaps they are right; after all, the Bible offers plenty of hope for Christians.

Are you happy for God to humble you?

a	2 Corinthians 13:5	Examine yourselves as to whether you are in the faith. Prove yourselves.
b	2 Peter 1:10	Therefore ... be even more diligent to make your calling and election sure, for if you do these things you will never stumble.
c	Revelation 3:17	... you say, 'I am rich, have become wealthy, and have need of nothing' ----- and do not know that you are wretched, miserable, poor, blind and naked
d	Luke 18:13	And the tax collector, standing afar off, would not so much as raise his eyes to heaven, but beat his breast, saying, 'God be merciful to me a sinner!'
e	Psalm 84:10	I would rather be a door-keeper in the house of my God than dwell in the tents of wickedness.
f	Proverbs 26:12	Do you see a man wise in his own eyes? There is more hope for a fool than for him.

Denying ourselves
(advisory)

Denying ourselves means giving up everything that does not please God. It means that you will not let yourself have anything that God dislikes, and so it is the opposite of living for what pleases you, the attitude we call selfishness. After all, everyone wants to please someone: ourselves, or somebody else. Christians live to please God, or at least they should. That does not mean that it is wrong to look after our own interests, so long as they are not our only interests. In fact, what pleases God is what is in our best interest.

Jesus Christ practised this kind of self-denial. He spent his whole life on earth doing what God his Father wanted. He never pleased himself.[a] And Christians try to live in the same way. They do not do what they want, but what they feel God wants.

Perhaps you are asking 'How much must I give up?' or trying to work out the exact figure. But it does not work like that. We are to deny ourselves whatever God wants denied[b], and all the while his life is in you, he will go on showing you what he wants. That means your self-denial will go on growing, and you will never reach the point in this life when self-denial is not needed any more. The more his life fills you, the more you want to please him, and the more it pleases you to want to please him.

Some people have denied themselves to make other people admire them. That is not self-denial at all. People like that are only pleasing themselves, by getting what they want, which is admiration. To test your self-denial, you need to ask yourself if you are as much concerned about Christ's work on earth as about your own; if you suffer when Christ is dishonoured; if you want his name to be more famous than your own.[c]

When you think about it, you realise that real self-denial is a good thing. It is stupid to want something God knows will not be any help to you. So if you do not deny yourself, then God will have to take it away from you, because he wants the best for you. He loves us enough to be stern with us when we go wrong, but it would be better to act first, and deny ourselves.[d]

a John 4:34		Jesus said to them, 'My food is to do the will of him who sent me, and to finish his work.'
b Luke 9:23		Then (Jesus) said to them all, 'If anyone desires to come after me, let him deny himself, and take up his cross daily, and follow me.
c John 3:30		He must increase but I must decrease.
d Hebrews 12:6		For whom the Lord loves he chastens, and scourges every son whom he receives.

Giving ourselves (advisory)

Denying ourselves is not enough. We must do it for a purpose, so that we can give ourselves to something else, or someone else. The best thing we can do is to deny ourselves so that we can give ourselves fully to God. Naturally, no one wants to do this, for we are too fond of ourselves. So anyone who does do it must have the new, spiritual life that God gives. Jesus Christ said, 'My food is to do the will of him who sent me and to finish his work.' He 'ate' God's will, and enjoyed it! So anyone else who does this must be one of Christ's people.

This does not mean that we stop doing our ordinary jobs, but it does mean that every day we think about God's work, and do not waste time doing work which is not pleasing him.

Real Christians give their time to God. They love Sundays because they can use that day to think about God and work for him in a special kind of way.[a] Real Christians are happy to give their possessions to God as well. They love to be generous.

Christians do not give themselves to God to make themselves pleasing to him, but because they want to serve him. Lovers do not kiss merely because they want kisses back, but to show their love. Are you giving something to God merely because you want to be rewarded? Or are you giving because you love him?[b]

Are these three advisory signs in our lives: humbling ourselves, denying ourselves, and giving ourselves?

a	Isaiah 58:13,14	If you turn away your foot from the Sabbath, from doing your pleasure on my holy day, and call the Sabbath a delight, the holy day of the Lord honourable, and shall honour him, not doing your own ways, nor finding your own pleasure, nor speaking your own words, then you shall delight yourself in the Lord.
b	1 Chronicles 29:5,9	Who then is willing to consecrate himself this day to the Lord? ... Then the people rejoiced, for they had offered willingly, because with a loyal heart they had offered willingly to the Lord.

Praying (informative)

We come now to the five informative signs, which show to people around us that we are Christians.[a] The first of these is praying.

We begin to pray when God's life comes into us, and this is one thing that others notice about us. Anybody can say a prayer: that of itself proves nothing. The sign of God's life in us is a prayerful spirit. A prayerful spirit is humble, because we know we do not deserve any answer at all; it is believing, because we know that Jesus died for us and will certainly listen to us; it is obedient, because we want what God wants; and it is sincere, because we know we cannot trick God by using fine words.

Some people say prayers to make themselves feel good, or to make other people think they are good, or to try and make themselves out to be Christians, or to still a nagging conscience, or because they think that God might just be pleased.[b] People like that do not seem to pray much in secret. They seem to need an audience, and they tend to give up if the audience gets too small.[c]

A prayerful spirit, however, prays in secret as well as in public, and becomes seriously alarmed if it does not feel like praying. Praying is like the soul breathing. A body is not alive unless it is breathing; the same goes for the soul. No real Christian ever stops praying. Have you started?

a	1 Peter 2:9	But you are a chosen generation; a royal priesthood, a holy nation, his own special people, that you may proclaim the praises of him who called you out of darkness into his marvellous light.
b	Luke 18:11	The Pharisee stood and prayed thus with himself, 'God, I thank you that I am not like other men ---- extortioners, unjust, adulterers, or even as this tax collector. I fast twice a week; I give tithes of all that I possess.
c	Matthew 6:5,6	And when you pray, you shall not be like the hypocrites. For they love to pray standing in the synagogues and on the corners of the street, that they may be seen by men. Assuredly, I say to you, they have their reward. But you, when you pray, go into your room, and when you have shut your door, pray to your Father who is in the secret place; and your Father, who sees in secret will reward you openly.

Sharing
(informative)

Real Christians stick together. They love all men because they are all made by God; but they have a special love for other Christians, because they are sons of God.[a]

You see, if God's life is in you, you will enjoy being with others who have God's life in them too. You will enjoy doing things together, and talking about your experiences of Jesus Christ. Christians call this 'fellowship', which means simply 'sharing', that is, sharing God's life in one another.[b] Real Christians rejoice to see the life of God in other Christians, because it reminds them of God himself. 'We know that we have passed from death to life' writes one of Christ's followers 'because we love our brothers.'[c] This is quite different from human love. Human love grows out of a human relationship; spiritual love can grow even where there is no human relationship. Real Christians love each other because God's life can be seen in them, and they want God to be known everywhere.[d]

This kind of love is a sign of God's life in man. Even when they upset one another, Christians simply cannot help loving one another: they all share God's life.

Do you share this love?

a	1 John 5:1	Whoever believes that Jesus is the Christ is born of God, and everyone who loves him who begot also loves him who is begotten of him.
b	Psalm 66:16	Come and hear, all you who fear God, and I will declare what he has done for my soul.
	Acts 2:44,45	Now all who believed were together, and had all things in common, and sold their possessions and goods and divided among them all, as anyone had need.
c	1 John 3:14	We know that we have passed from death to life, because we love the brethren. He who does not love his brother abides in death.
d	John 13:35	By this all will know that you are my disciples, if you have love for one another.

Separating
(informative)

God's life in real Christians makes them different from other people. As we have seen, it makes them humble, self-denying and self-giving. This is very different from the way non-Christians behave, and real Christians are bound to be different. Christians sometimes explain this by saying they are 'separate from the world'. Jesus warned his followers that the world would hate them just as it had hated him. The world had crucified him and might crucify them too.[a]

Non-Christians hate the things which Christians love; they want the things which Christians leave alone; they behave in ways Christians will not; they are careless about things that matter to Christians, and anxious about things that do not trouble Christians. A Christian is different. If he is not, he is not a Christian.[b] It is true that Christians sometimes behave like non-Christians, but only if they are unhealthy Christians or imitation Christians. If there is no difference between us and the world, then there must be real doubt if we are Christians at all.

The non-Christian lives for the things of this world: what else can he do? The Christian lives for the world to come: what else would you expect?[c] The Bible tells us that if anyone loves the world, that is, if he has nothing else to live for, the love of God is not in him.[d] It is as simple as that.

Has anyone noticed that you are different?[e]

a John 15:18

If the world hates you, you know that it hated me before it hated you.

b Ephesians 2:1-3,10

And you he made alive, who were dead in trespasses and sins, in which you once walked according to the course of this world according to the prince of the power of the air, the spirit who now works in the sons of disobedience, among whom also we all once conducted ourselves in the lusts of our flesh, fulfilling the desires of the flesh and of the mind, and were by nature children of wrath, just as the others ... For we are his workmanship, created in Christ Jesus for good works, which God prepared beforehand that we should walk in them.

c Philippians 3:18-21

For many walk, of whom I have told you often, and now tell you even weeping, that they are the enemies of the cross of Christ whose end is destruction, whose god is their belly, and whose glory is in their shame — who set their mind on earthly things. For our citizenship is in heaven, from which we so eagerly wait for the Saviour, the Lord Jesus Christ, who will transform our lowly body that it may be conformed to his glorious body, according to the working by which he is able even to subdue all things to himself.

d 1 John 2:15

Do not love the world or the things in the world. If anyone loves the world, the love of the Father is not in him.

e 1 Peter 4:3,4

For we have spent enough of our past lifetime in doing the will of the Gentiles — when we walked in licentiousness, lusts, drunkenness, revelries, drinking parties and abominable idolatries. In regard to these, they think it strange that you do not run with them to the same excess, speaking evil of you.

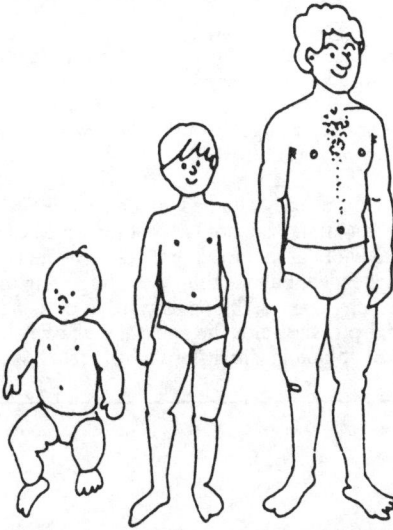

Growing
(informative)

A cell becomes a baby, then a child, then a youth, then an adult. A seed produces a shoot and a root, and grows into a complete plant which produces fruit. All living things grow.

Real Christians grow too. They have God's life in them, so they ought to grow in God's way. A real Christian is a growing Christian. Imitation Christians never grow. They just go on acting the same part over and over again, and are perfectly content to stay as they are.[a]

Real Christians are never content to stay as they are. They want more and more of God; they hate their own sins more and more; they love Christ more and more; they fight the devil more and more; they grow more and more hungry for the Bible; they become more and more eager for Christian fellowship; they trust more and more in the power of prayer. They experience struggles, stumbles, mistakes and muddles; they see clouds as well as clear skies; but it's always like that with growing things. If something is alive, it will go on growing. Only the dead give up growing.

Real Christians never give up growing because it is God's life that makes them grow. God never gives up, so if you are not a Christian now, you never were one. And if you ever were a real Christian, you are still one, and always will be. God always finishes what he begins.[b] He does not put his life into a person and then change his mind and take it out again. So what about you: are you still growing?[c]

If something in your life is stopping you growing properly, hunt it out and kill it! Or if your growth is being hindered by something you should have outgrown by now, get rid of it! After all, an adult cannot wear the clothes he wore as a baby.

a	2 Peter 3:18	... grow in the grace and knowledge of our Lord and Saviour Jesus Christ. To him be the glory both now and for ever.
b	Philippians 1:6	... he who has begun a good work in you will complete it until the day of Jesus Christ.
c	Philippians 3:12-14	Not that I have already attained, or am already perfected; but I press on, that I may lay hold of that for which Christ Jesus has also laid hold of me. Brethren, I do not count myself to have apprehended; but one thing I do, forgetting those things which are behind and reaching forward to those things which are ahead, I press towards the goal for the prize of the upward call of God in Christ Jesus.

Obeying
(informative)

Good trees produce good fruit, and bad trees produce bad fruit. In the same way, a person's behaviour shows what kind of person he is.[a] If a man really belongs to Christ, his behaviour will be Christlike. The life of God in him will show. Anyone who says he loves God should test himself carefully. Does he do what God wants? If not, his love of God is not real.[b]

The best thing anyone can do is to obey God. There is nothing higher or more holy: it is the very top of the Christian ladder. And this obedience involves obeying all God's commands, those that refer to God and those that refer to our fellow-men. It involves obeying God's commands all of the time, not just sometimes. Real Christians don't always achieve this, but when they fail, they are truly sorry; they desperately want not to fail.[c] That is the difference between the real Christians and the imitation Christians or non-Christians.

Obedience also involves keeping all God's commands with enthusiasm, even when it is dangerous to do so, for the Christian wants to be just like Jesus Christ, who was perfect to the bitter end. His first followers tried to do the same, and so do all real Christians; for Christianity is not a set of ideas or ideals, but a power that changes people and makes them more obedient to God.[d]

a	Matthew 7:16-20	You will know them by their fruits. Do men gather grapes from thorn bushes or figs from thistles? Even so, every good tree bears good fruit, but a bad tree bears bad fruit. A good tree cannot bear bad fruit, nor can a bad tree bear good fruit. Every tree that does not bear good fruit is cut down and thrown into the fire. Therefore by their fruits you will know them.
b	John 14:21	He who has my commandments and keeps them, it is he who loves me.
c	1 John 3:9	Whoever has been born of God does not sin. (No one who is born of God practices sin. NASB version).
d	1 Peter 1:14,15	... as obedient children, not conforming yourselves to the former lusts, as in your ignorance; but as he who called you is holy, you also be holy in all your conduct.

Part Three
What's the Verdict?

The real thing?

You can test yourself now! As I said at the beginning, this book is to help you do just that. It simply repeats the tests God himself lays down in the Bible.[a] These are the tests God will use on everyone some day. He will not change them. He does not need to. If you choose to ignore these tests now, you will have to face them then. So it would be sensible to check them yourself now, while there is time.

A person either has the life of God in him or he does not. If he has, he can know.[b] If he has not, he can ask.[c] It could hardly be fairer than that; but it is important not to be deceived by wrong ideas, which is why this book sets out to tell you God's ideas. There is no heaven for the man without God's life in him.

Some readers may be real Christians who are troubled by doubts. You can answer your doubts by examining yourself in the light of these tests. Your doubts are a sign of life. Dead things do not doubt. If you have enough of God's life in you to cry out 'God, have mercy on me, a sinner', you have good reason to be glad. The Lord Jesus has a special love for people like you.

Other readers may already be strong Christians. You can become even stronger by giving yourself more and more to God. He bought you for himself. Give him what he owns: all of you. Nothing else is the real thing.

a	Acts 17:11	... these were more fair-minded than those in Thessalonica, in that they received the word with all readiness, and searched the Scriptures daily to find out whether these things were so. Therefore many of them believed ...
b	1 John 5:20	We know that the Son of God has come and has given us an understanding, that we may know him who is true;
c	Acts 16:30-31	'Sirs, what must I do to be saved?' So they said, 'Believe on the Lord Jesus Christ, and you will be saved, you and your household.'

An after-word

Some books have more than one author. Perhaps two people get together to write a book between them, or a number of people put a book together by writing a chapter each, or somebody finishes a book begun by someone else. This book has had no less than five authors, and has taken over 250 years to reach its present form.

First was Jonathan Edwards, who was a minister in America in the Eighteenth Century. In 1734 and 1735, and again in 1740, large numbers of people in the town where he lived became Christians in the course of what we call a 'revival'. However, after a few years Edwards noticed that some of those who had apparently become Christians had gone back to their old ways. He realised that they had never been Christians at all, but had only been imitating the way Christians behave. So he wrote a book with the strange title of *The Religious Affections*, to show the difference between real and imitation Christians.

Second was another American preacher, Gardiner Spring. He wrote a book called *The Distinguishing Traits of Christian Character*, which seems to have been based on Edwards' book, though it is much shorter and easier to read.

Third were A. N. Martin and E. C. Reisinger and fourth were H. J. Appleby and J. K. Davies, whose shortened and simplified version of Spring's book, *What's Real?*, was published in 1978.

I come last of all. The present work is a rewriting of *What's Real?* I have endeavoured to smooth down the English to make for easier reading, but the substance of the book is virtually unchanged. May it continue to be as useful in its new form as its three predecessors. *'The Religious Affections'* is available in the Grace Publications Condensed Classics series, No 11 — *The experience that counts'*.

Philip Tait
St John's Wood, 1993
London